Contents

Chapter 1
The Basics

What is Microsoft PowerPoint?

Microsoft PowerPoint is the leading graphics presentation package. You can use it to create, design and organise professional presentations quickly and easily.

Getting started

 Load **Microsoft PowerPoint.** You can do this in one of two ways:

 Either double-click the **PowerPoint** icon

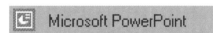 Or click **Start** at the bottom left of the screen, then click **Programs,** then click

Microsoft PowerPoint

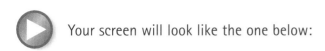 Your screen will look like the one below:

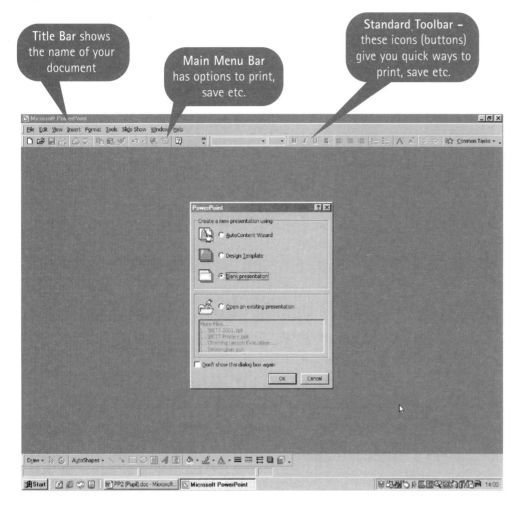

Title Bar shows the name of your document

Main Menu Bar has options to print, save etc.

Standard Toolbar – these icons (buttons) give you quick ways to print, save etc.

Figure 1.1: The opening screen

The AutoContent Wizard

The **New Presentation** dialogue box appears automatically at the start of a new session in **PowerPoint.** This is the smaller window in the picture above.

The **AutoContent Wizard** is the quickest way to produce a simple presentation because it does all the planning for you.

In this chapter you will use it to produce a simple presentation advertising a school sports day.

 Make sure the **AutoContent Wizard** is selected.

 Click **OK.**

You will see the dialogue box shown in Figure 1.2 below:

Figure 1.2: The AutoContent Wizard dialogue box

The flowchart on the left of the screen shows you that you are at the **Start**, and in the next few dialogue boxes you will be asked to choose a **Presentation type, style** and so on. Keep your eye on the green box in the flowchart, which tells you where you are.

▶ Click **Next** to go to the next dialogue box, where you will choose a **Presentation type.**

▶ Select **General** from the list of buttons.

▶ Click **Generic** in the right hand list box and then click **Next.**

Figure 1.3: Selecting a Presentation type

The **Presentation style** dialogue box asks how you would like to present your information. Select **On-Screen presentation.** Click **Next.**

In the **Presentation options** dialogue box enter **'School Sports Day'** as the presentation title. Uncheck the **Date last updated** and **Slide number** options.

Figure 1.4: Presentation options

Once you have entered your details, click **Next.** Click **Finish** to build your presentation.

You will then see your presentation in **Normal View** with the topics shown in **Outline.** (The **Status bar** at the bottom of the screen tells you this.)

Your title screen appears in a **Presentation window** in the right hand corner of your screen. This is how it will look when it is run. The text on the left of the screen is the skeleton of your presentation.

Figure 1.5: The Presentation in Normal view

Viewing the Presentation

Want to see the show so far?

 Click the **Slide Show** icon (see figure 1.5)

 Click the mouse to go to the next slide. You'll see that this slide and all the others need to be edited by you.

Press **Escape** to stop viewing the slides and return to **Normal View.**

Adding your own content

The suggested topics for each slide might be useful for a future presentation, but they are not much help here. You need to have a plan in your head or on paper of what you are going to put on each slide. This time, that's been done for you!

 Highlight the heading text 'Introduction' on Slide 2 by dragging the mouse pointer over the word or double-clicking it. This can be done on the text in either the Outline Pane or the Slide Pane.

 Replace the highlighted text with the following: '10th Annual Junior Games'.

 Replace the next two lines with the time and date: '12:00 – 4:00pm on the 25th of June', and the location: 'On the Main Field'.

 On slide 1, delete Default.

 On Slide 3, replace the heading text with 'Events'. Replace the text on the following line with '100, 200 & 400 Metres' and then press Enter.

Pressing Enter will give you another blank line in which to type in another event.

 Enter two more events of your choice.

Note:
The text changes to **Click to Add Subtitle** but only in Design View.

Deleting unwanted slides

 Select Slides 4-9 ready to be deleted. To do this hold your mouse pointer just before the T of Topic 1 on Slide 4 and drag down across the text to the bottom.

 You can then delete the unwanted slides by selecting Edit, Delete Slide, or by pressing the Delete Key.

Now you have finished your presentation. Click the **Slide Show** icon to view it. Click the mouse to change slides.

Your presentation should look like the one in Figure 1.6.

Figure 1.6: The finished slides

Saving your presentation

Click **File** on the menu bar and select **Save.** Save it as **Sports.ppt** – you don't need to type the file extension **.ppt,** which **PowerPoint** will add automatically.

You can now close the file without losing your work by selecting **File, Close** from the menu.

Chapter 2
Template Wizard

Over the next several chapters you'll be working on a longer presentation. It is the sort of topic that you might be asked to prepare and deliver in one of your classes at school. Having **PowerPoint** to help you will make it a whole lot easier to prepare and deliver!

Project: Prepare a slide presentation to be delivered on a computer screen on the topic of 'Building styles in the village of Coddenham'.

Planning a presentation

To deliver an effective presentation you need to consider who your audience is, and prepare your slides to suit them. The audience could be your classmates, your teachers or even the general public at an Open Day.

Whoever your presentation is for, here are a few basic guidelines:

Start with a title screen showing what the project is about.

Don't put more than 4 or 5 points on each slide. People can't concentrate on too much information at once.

Keep each point short and simple. You may want to talk around each point to explain it in further detail.

Sound, graphics and animation can add interest, but don't overdo them!

The Template Wizard

You have already seen the **AutoContent wizard.** Another way to create a quick and colourful presentation is to use a **Design Template.**

 Load **Microsoft PowerPoint.** You will see the following screen:

Note:

If **PowerPoint** is already running, select **File, New,** from the menu and click on the **Design Templates** tab.

Figure 2.1: Selecting the Template Wizard

 Select **Design Template** and click **OK.**

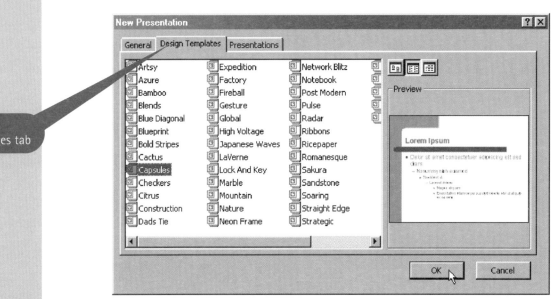

Design Templates tab

Figure 2.2: The Design Templates tab and selected design

Select the **Capsules** template and click **OK.**

 In the **New Slide** dialogue box, choose the first **AutoLayout** from the selection. This is a Title Slide and is the most suitable layout for the first page of your new presentation.

Figure 2.3: Various layout options

 Click **OK.**

 Save your new blank presentation as **Buildings.ppt**

Placeholders

Each slide layout displays **placeholders** that allow you to easily add objects such as text, a clip art image or a chart to a slide. You will see some examples of these on the Title Slide.

Tip:
It is always important to save your work at regular intervals to make sure that you don't lose too much if something unexpected happens, such as a power cut.

Adding text to the title screen

 Click the Title placeholder (where **PowerPoint** tells you to click) and type the title **'Building styles in the village of Coddenham'**.

 Now add a sub-title. Click where indicated, and type: **'An historical look at building styles through the ages'**.

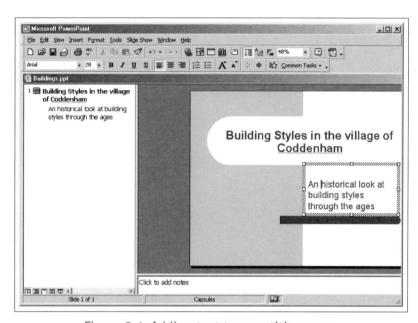

Figure 2.4: Adding text to your title screen

Formatting and moving the text

You can click the text boxes to move them around the screen. You can also format the text in each text box – for example, change its colour, size or alignment.

To format text you need to select the text box by clicking its border. When the border has changed from a diagonal striped box to a fuzzy one you know you can start formatting the text.

If you want to edit, add or delete text in a box, click inside the box. The border changes to diagonal stripes.

Figure 2.5: Formatting box pattern

Select the sub-title text box.

Centre the sub-title by clicking on the **Centre** button.

Now make the text Italic by clicking on the **Italic** button.

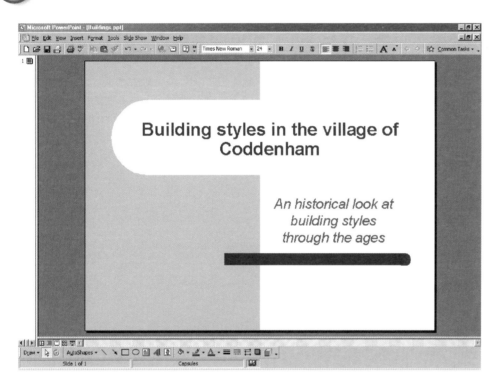

Figure 2.6: The title screen in Slide view

Changing the view

You can alternate between various views of the presentation by clicking on the icons at the bottom of the screen.

Normal View

This is the most useul view as it lets you see the structure of your presentation down the left of the screen and the current slide you are working on. This is the view currently selected and shown in Figure 2.4.

Slide View

This view enlarges the Slide pane of the **Normal View** and allows you to view one entire slide as it would be displayed during a presentation. It is most useful for editing and formatting text. This is the view currently selected and shown in Figure 2.6.

Outline View

This view enlarges the Outline pane of the **Normal View**. Try clicking on it to see what happens. You can also edit text in this mode and view all your screens in the right hand presentation window by clicking on the slide headings.

 Click the **Outline View** button at the bottom of the screen.

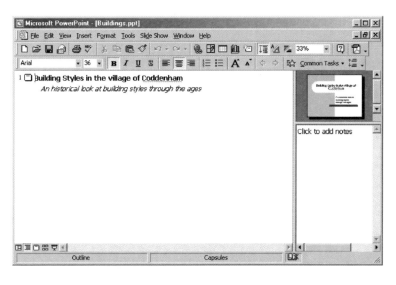

Figure 2.7: The title screen in Outline view

Slide Sorter View

This view helps you to organise your slides in later stages. We'll be looking at this view later when you have more than one slide. Here's a preview of what it will look like when you have 6 slides:

Figure 2.8: Slide Sorter view

Slide Show

Click this icon to view your presentation.

Save and close the presentation.

Tip:
You will be returned to the previously selected view after the last slide has been shown. You can press **Escape** (the key marked **Esc**) at any time during a presentation to end it.

Chapter 3
Editing a Show

In this chapter you'll add some more to the presentation you started in Chapter 2. You will also be able to change the order of your bullet points and swap the slides around.

Opening an existing presentation

▶ Load **PowerPoint.**

▶ Select **Open an existing presentation.** Click **OK.**

▶ Note: If **PowerPoint** is already running, click **File, Open...** on the main menu.

Figure 3.1: Opening an existing presentation

If you cannot see your filename, you can click the small downward arrow in the **Look In:** box. This will bring up a list of folders for you to search.

 Click the **Buildings.ppt** file that you created earlier and click **Open**.

 Make sure you are in Normal view by pressing the **Normal View** button at the bottom of the screen.

Starting a new slide

Now you can begin the second slide of the presentation.

 Click the **New Slide** icon on the Standard toolbar.

 The second layout, **Bulleted List** is already selected for you by **PowerPoint.** Click **OK.**

Enter the text as on the following screenshot, remembering to press **Enter** each time you need to start a new point.

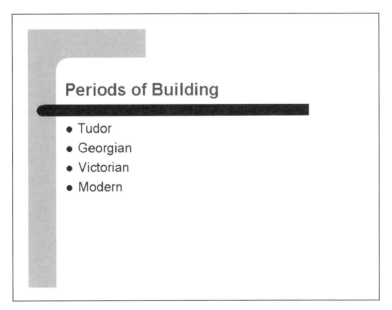

Figure 3.2: Slide 2

Changing text size

You can increase or decrease the size of the text by using the **Font Size** button on the Formatting toolbar. **PowerPoint** also has special buttons for shrinking or enlarging the font one size at a time.

 Select all of the bulleted text on the current slide.

 Click several times on the **Increase Font Size** button to increase the size of the text. The button is located towards the right hand end of the Formatting toolbar.

Your screen should now look something like the one below. (The text in this screen has been enlarged four or five times.)

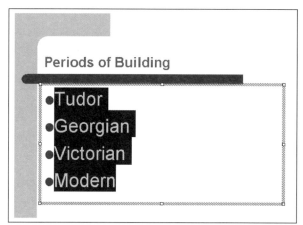

Figure 3.3: Increasing the size of the text

Checking your spelling

You can check your spelling either by using the main menu commands or by clicking the **Spelling and Grammar** button, which you will now do.

 Click the **Spelling and Grammar** button on the left of the Standard toolbar.

 PowerPoint will try to correct all the words it has underlined in red. It should find **Coddenham.** Don't change this to **codename!**

 Close the dialogue box.

The Outlining toolbar

 Click the **Outline View** button to go to Outline View.

Look at your screen. Does it have a toolbar down the left hand side, like the one shown in Figure 3.8? If not, you need to display it now.

 From the menu, select **View, Toolbars.** Select **Outlining.**

The Outlining toolbar will appear.

Tip:
A quick way to display the Outlining toolbar is to right-click any button and click **Outlining** on the pop-up menu.

Adding more slides

The next four slides are going to show more detail about each of these styles of building.

Note:

PowerPoint 97 allowed you to select **Tools, Expand Slide** from the menu. This would automatically have produced the extra four slides.

 Make sure you are in Outline view.

 Click the **New Slide** icon on the Standard toolbar.

 Select the **Bulleted List** layout as before and click **OK**.

 Type **Tudor** as the slide title in the Outline Pane. Press **Enter**.

A new slide should appear.

 Type in the next 3 slide titles, **Georgian**, **Victorian**, **Modern**, pressing **Enter** between each one.

Emma, Fee and Robin are having fun with the spell checker. They have typed in their school friend's name **Gary Payne**.

You should now have four new slides, each with their own headings as shown in the Outline pane below.

1 ☐ **Building styles in the village of Coddenham**
An historical look at building styles through the ages
2 ☐ **Periods of Building**
- Tudor
- Georgian
- Victorian
- Modern
3 ☐ **Tudor**
4 ☐ **Georgian**
5 ☐ **Victorian**
6 ☐ **Modern**

Figure 3.4

Select the third slide by double-clicking its **Slide** icon. ──────── 3 ☐

Add text to this slide. Type '**Characteristics of a Tudor house**' where indicated on the slide and press **Enter**.

Now press the **Tab** key or click the **Demote** button to indent the next point. Demote means 'to make less important'.

The Promote and Demote buttons

Tip:
If you are ever unsure about what a button does, hold your mouse pointer over it for a second and a **Tool Tip** will appear telling you what the button is called.

Your screen should now look like this:

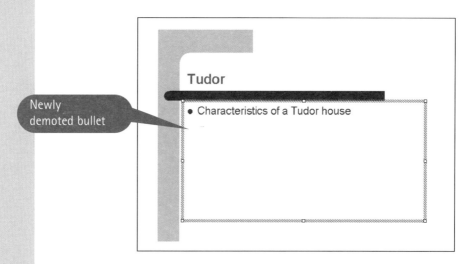

Figure 3.5: Demoting new bullet points

Customising bullets

You can change the style and colour of bullets to increase the impact of a subset of points.

 Click the new line and select **Format, Bullets and Numbering...** on the menu.

 With the **Bulleted** tab selected, click **Character...** in the bottom right corner of the window.

The Bullet window will appear.

 Select a new shape for your bullet. Click **OK**.

Figure 3.6: Changing the appearance of bullets

Note:

This will only affect the style of bullets on this slide. To change the style of bullets throughout the presentation you should use the menu option **View, Master, Slide Master**. You can experiment with this later in your own presentations!

The bullet will change to its proper colour as soon as you type some text. Type **External** and then press **Enter.**

Press the **Tab** key or click the **Demote** button to indent the next point.

Type the three external features as shown in Figure 3.7.

Click the **Promote** button before typing **Internal.**

Click the **Demote** button and then type the rest of the text as shown below.

Figure 3.7: Demoting points – Levels 1, 2 and 3

Moving text lines around

The Tudor feature, **'Small windows'** could also be under the **Internal** heading. Move it down to its new place as follows:

 Click the mouse pointer to the left of **'Small windows'** in the Outline pane and you will see a four-headed arrow style pointer.

 Hold the mouse down and begin to drag downwards. A line will appear across the text. Keep going down until the line is underneath **'Low ceilings'** and let go.

Tip:
If the headings are not shown, double-click on the slide icon in the Outline pane.

Outlining toolbar

Slide icon

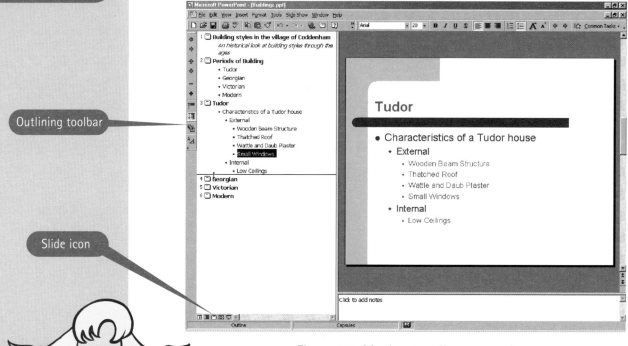

Figure 3.8: Moving text lines around

Tip:
An alternative way to move text up or down is to select the line and then click the **Move Up** or **Move Down** buttons on the Outlining toolbar. To see this toolbar, right-click any other button and click **Outlining**.

The text should have moved down the slide. You can move text from one slide to another in the same way.

 Click to the left of **Characteristics of a Tudor house.** Everything in this paragraph will automatically be selected.

 Drag downwards to put the text into the slide for **Georgian.**

 You don't really want it there, so click **Undo.** The **Undo** button is on the Standard toolbar at the top of your screen.

Changing the order of slides

 Try moving Slide 4, **Georgian** to below Slide 5, **Modern.**

 Click **Undo.**

Hint:
Click and drag
the **Slide 4** icon.

Checking your presentation

You can view your progress so far. Look at it first in Slide Sorter view.

 Click the **Slide Sorter View** button at the bottom of the screen.

When you click the **Slide Show** button, the presentation starts at the selected slide (the one with a black border).

 Click the first slide to select it.

  Click the **Slide Show** button at the bottom of the screen.

Click or press the **Space bar** to move to the next slide. (Pressing the **Backspace** key goes back one slide. Remember you can exit your presentation at any time by pressing the **Esc** key.)

Take a break!

  Save your work using the **Save** icon.

Close the presentation.

Chapter **4**
Applying Designs

Now you're ready to think more about the overall appearance of your slides. Some slides may need a brighter background than others to increase their impact, or you may want to change the design template. Whatever your ideas, **PowerPoint** has many functions for customising the way you want your slides to look.

Changing the Design Template

 Select **File, Open** to open the file named **Buildings.ppt.**

 Select **Format, Apply Design Template...** from the menu.

Figure 4.1: Selecting a new Design Template

Choose the **Lock And Key.pot** design. You will notice that the **Capsules.pot** design is the one you chose when you first began your project.

 Click **Apply.**

Changing the Slide Colour Scheme

 Note:
In some **PowerPoint** designs, the Title slide has a graphic which is not displayed on the other slides.

 With any slide selected, choose **Format, Slide Colour Scheme...** from the menu.

Figure 4.2: Changing the slide colour scheme

 Select the bottom-right design and click the **Apply to All** button.

You can also try customising your own slide using the **Custom** tab.

Tip:
This changes the colour scheme in all the slides. To change just the selected slide, click **Apply** instead of **Apply to All.**

Changing the background styles and colours

It is possible to change the styles and colours of the backgrounds in your slides without making any changes to the text colours or designs.

 In Normal view, select Slide 1 by clicking on its icon in the ──────── Outline pane.

 Choose **Format, Background** from the menu bar.

 Now click the small **down-arrow** beside the 'colour' box.

Figure 4.3: Changing the slide background

 Click **Fill Effects...** from the drop-down menu.

Figure 4.4: Applying a One Color gradient effect to a slide background

Tip:
You can scroll through all your slides using the scroll bar.

 With the **Gradient** tab selected, click **One Color.**

 Change **Color 1** to the medium brown colour by clicking the downward facing arrow in the **Color 1** box and click **OK.**

 Click **Apply.** This will change the background on just the Title slide because it was pre-selected earlier.

Tip:
Try experimenting with some of the various settings in the **Fill Effects** window such as the Colors and Shading Styles available.

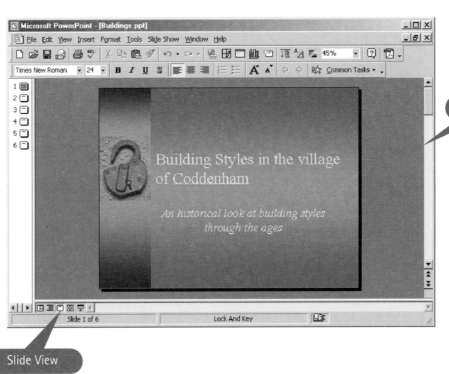

Figure 4.5: The new Title screen background

You can also add textures or patterns to your slides in the same way by clicking on the **Texture** or **Pattern** tabs (See Figure 4.4).

If you have a picture of your own that you would like to see as a background for your slide, you can add it by selecting the **Picture** tab. (This is an advanced feature which will not be covered in this book.)

Changing the layout of a slide

PowerPoint allows you to choose between a number of layouts for each slide. Some layouts are suitable for slides with bullet points, others for slides which will include clip art or photographs, and others for slides showing charts or graphs.

 In Normal view, select the fourth slide titled **Georgian.**

 To select a new layout choose **Format, Slide Layout...**

 Select the layout named **2 Column Text** as shown below. Click **Apply.**

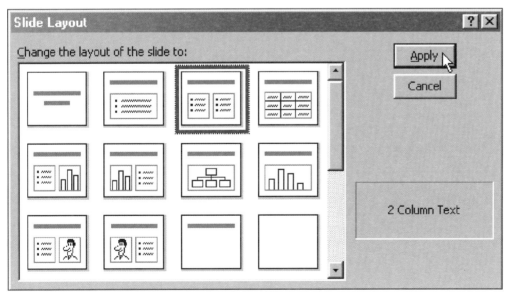

Figure 4.6: Selecting a new layout

Click the **Slide View** icon to see your changes!

Tip:
It is important to select the correct layout for a slide before you add any objects. An **object** is usually a picture or chart.

On the slide, enter the text as shown below.

Your screen should now look like this.

Figure 4.7: Column Text

 Make the text bigger by selecting it and clicking the **Increase Font Size** button.

Choosing a layout to include Clip Art

The fifth slide will have a picture as well as text, so first you must change its layout.

 In Outline view, select the fifth slide titled **Victorian.**

 Click **Format, Slide Layout...**

 Select the layout named **Text & Clip Art** as shown below. Click **Apply.**

Figure 4.8: Text & Clip Art Layout

You will learn how to use Clip Art in the next chapter.

 Save and close your presentation.

Chapter 5
Adding Objects

You can add pictures, scanned photographs or cartoons to your documents. You can even put in graphs and charts.

 If it is not already on screen, open the presentation called **Buildings.ppt.**

 In Normal view, double-click the fifth Slide icon and press the **Slide View** button to view the **Victorian** slide.

Tip:
In Slide view you can scroll through the slides.

Figure 5.1: Slide 5 in Slide view

Click where indicated to add text and type **'External Features'**. Press **Enter.**

 Press the **Tab** key or click the **Demote** button. Add the sub-points: ———
Sash Windows, Decorated Bargeboard and **White Brick Construction.**

Changing spacing

Instead of increasing text size to fill the slide, you can increase the spacing between the three points.

 Highlight the text and click the **Increase Paragraph Spacing** button ———
on the Formatting toolbar.

Figure 5.2: Increasing paragraph spacing

 With the text still selected, press the **Increase Font Size** button.

 Adjust the spacing again if necessary.

Inserting a Clip Art image

You may have a CD with some clip art you can use. Clip art is simply a collection of pictures and drawings that have been drawn by professional artists and collected together for other people to use. **PowerPoint** comes with a small collection of clip art.

 Double-click where shown (on the **Clip Art placeholder**) to add a clip art image.

 Select the **Buildings** category and choose the **Victorian Street Scene** picture. Click **OK**.

Tip:

Not there? Click on **Keep Looking** below to see the next screen.

Figure 5.3: Choosing a Clip Art image

Click this button to insert the clip art image

Note:

The range of clip art available with the **PowerPoint** package is fairly narrow. In this example a street scene has been used to help you imagine a real Victorian house, but you may find something better. You may also have a slightly different selection of pictures to choose from. A good place to find clip art pictures is on the Internet on Microsoft's On-Line Clip Art Gallery at **www.microsoft.com/clipgallerylive**.

The picture of the street scene will appear on your slide.

Figure 5.4

The Picture toolbar may appear when the graphic is selected.

Handles

 Note the little squares surrounding the graphic (picture). These are called handles. When the handles are visible, the graphic is **selected.**

 Click away from the graphic and the handles disappear.

 Click anywhere inside the graphic and the handles will be visible again.

Changing the size of the graphic

You can make the graphic bigger or smaller without changing its proportions by dragging any of the corner handles.

 Make sure the graphic is selected so that the handles are visible.

 Move the pointer over the middle left handle until it is shaped like a horizontal two-headed arrow.

 Click and hold down the left mouse button. The pointer changes to a cross-hair.

 Drag outwards. A dotted rectangle shows how big the graphic will be when you release the mouse button. When it is about 1cm wider, release the button.

 Save your work so far.

Adding a chart

Slide 6 would be created in a similar way. You can complete Slide 6 on your own if you have time, putting in some features of a modern house and maybe some suitable clip art.

Next, add a new slide to put a graph on.

  Click the **Slide Sorter View** button in the bottom left of your screen.

 Select the final slide by clicking on it.

Add a new slide by one of the following methods: click the **New Slide** icon, or use the menu option **Insert, New Slide...** or click **New Slide** on the Common Tasks toolbar (see Figure 5.5).

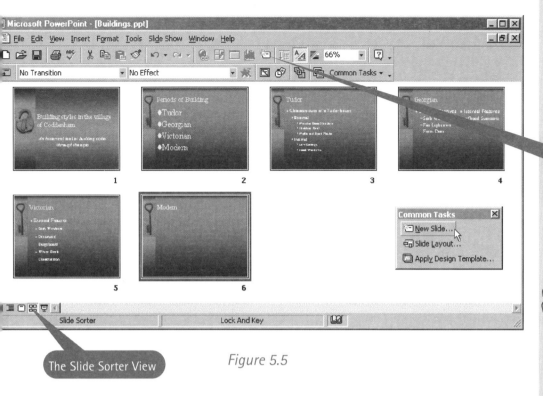

New Slide icon

The Slide Sorter View

Figure 5.5

On this new slide you are going to create a chart to show the number of Tudor, Georgian and Victorian houses in Coddenham.

 Select the **Chart** layout from the slide choices.

Figure 5.6: The Chart layout

 Click **OK**.

 With the slide selected, click the **Slide View** button.

Tip:
You can drag **Common Tasks** off the main toolbar above.

39

Now you are ready to begin making your chart.

 Double-click the chart placeholder that **PowerPoint** has created on the slide.

You will then see a small spreadsheet like you would see in Microsoft Excel. Notice that some of the icons on the Standard toolbar have changed.

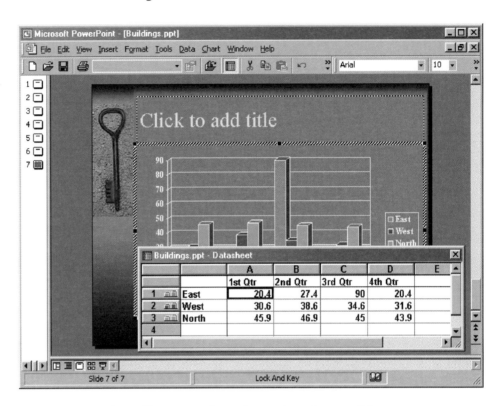

Figure 5.7: Inserting a chart into a slide

To make your chart you need to add your own information into the table.

 Click once in the cell labelled **East.**

 Now begin typing **Tudor.** This will replace **East** with **Tudor.**

 Click in each cell and type the row headings **Georgian** and **Victorian** and numbers shown in Figure 5.8.

 Make columns A, B and C wider by dragging the border between column headers.

Type the column headings **Village Centre, Main Village** and **Outskirts.**

 Delete column **D** by clicking the column header and pressing the **Delete** key.

Figure 5.8: Data in the datasheet

 Close the table by pressing the **Close** icon. ———————————— ✕

 Title your chart: **Number of Period Houses in Coddenham.**

 Click away from the heading to view the finished article.

 PowerPoint does not recognise the word **Coddenham,** so it underlines it. Right-click it and select **Ignore All.**

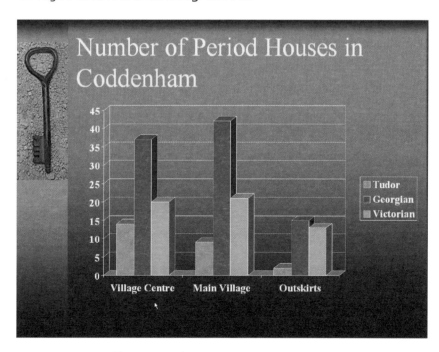

Figure 5.9: Slide featuring chart

Editing a chart

Suppose you have made a mistake in one of the figures or headings in the chart.

 Double-click the chart. The datasheet appears again.

 Make any changes you want in the datasheet. The chart changes automatically.

Tip:
If the datasheet does not appear when you double-click the chart, select **View**, **Datasheet** from the menu.

 Click away from the datasheet and it will disappear.

Wrapping up

 Click the **Slide Sorter View** button. This will let you see your presentation as a whole and organise your slides.

Suppose you have decided that you no longer need to explain what a modern house looks like, but would like to add a concluding slide.

 Move the **Modern** slide to the end. To do this **click** and **drag** the slide until a vertical line appears. Release the mouse button when the line is on the right hand side of the final slide.

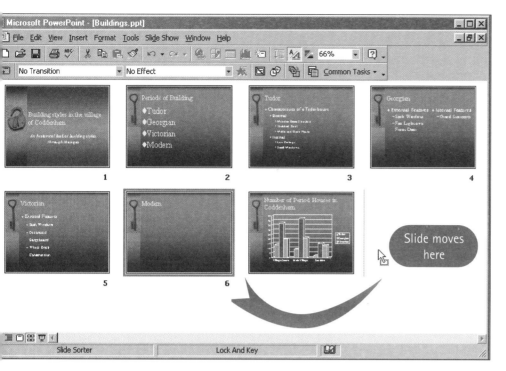

Figure 5.10: Moving slides in Slide Sorter View

In Normal view, replace **Modern** with **The End.** You can also thank your audience for coming if you wish.

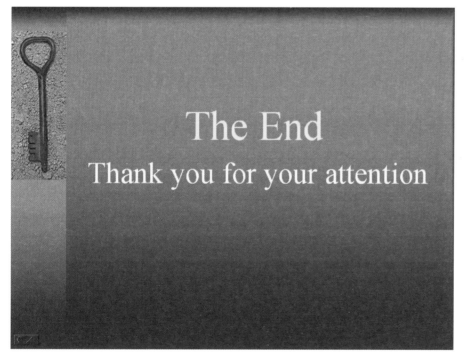

Figure 5.11: Concluding your presentation

To get rid of the bullet points on this slide, deselect the **Bullets** button on the toolbar.

Centre the text.

Save and **Close** your presentation.

43

Chapter 6
Special Effects

In this chapter you will be adding sounds and animation to a presentation. You can also add transition effects when each screen opens.

Multimedia objects and effects, such as pictures, animation and sounds help to keep the attention of your audience.

 Open the presentation **Buildings.ppt.**

 Select the **Slide Sorter View** and click the first slide.

Viewing a slide show

Before you add any special effects to a show, it is a good idea to view it as it is. This helps you to build a picture in your mind of what it needs to jazz it up a little.

 Click the **Slide Show** button beside the Slide Sorter View button.

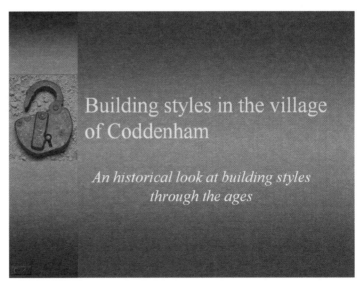

Figure 6.1: Slide 1 in Slide Show view

Click the mouse to change to the next slide.

 Keep going until **PowerPoint** returns you to the **Slide Sorter** view.

Adding slide transitions

Transitions change the way a slide opens. You can make the next slide open like a blind or a curtain, for example.

You will notice that in **Slide Sorter** view a new Slide Sorter toolbar appears at the top of the screen. This has all the tools for adding transitions and effects to your slides.

Figure 6.2: The Slide Sorter toolbar

 With the first slide selected, click the **Slide Transition** icon at the left hand end of this toolbar.

A slide transition window opens:

Figure 6.3: Selecting a Slide Transition

Scroll down the list and select **Split Vertical Out.** This will make the first screen open like a curtain, as if it were opening in a cinema.

You can also change the speed at which the transition occurs. In most cases, **Fast** is the best. Try experimenting!

 Click **Apply.**

 You will notice a small icon appear underneath the slide. This represents a transition action on that slide.

 View your changes by clicking the **Slide Show** button.

 You can also view your presentation in Slide Sorter View by clicking the **Animation Preview** button.

Tip:
If you click the right hand mouse button while you are viewing your show, you can select **End Show** to stop it. Or, you can simply press the **Esc** key.

Adding transitions to multiple slides

If you wish to add a transition to all the slides, you need only click the **Apply to All** button in the Slide Transition selection box.

You can apply a transition to more than one slide but not all by selecting them first using the **Ctrl** key, or **Shift** to select a range.

To add the same transition to all the rest of the slides:

 Make sure that you are in **Slide Sorter View.**

 Click Slide 2 and then hold down the **Shift** key.

 With the **Shift** key still pressed, click Slide 7.

Figure 6.4: Selecting multiple slides

▶ Click the **Slide Transition** button.

▶ Choose the **Cover Left** transition.

▶ Click **Apply.**

▶ **View** your show.

Adding Sounds

You can add a sound to accompany the transition. For example if you have a slide that pops in from one side, you could put a 'whoosh' sound in there.

▶ Click the **Slide Transition** button. ──────────────── 🔁

▶ Under the **Sound** choices, select **Whoosh.**

▶ Click **Apply to All.**

You can try out different sounds to see which ones you like.

Adding special effects to text

PowerPoint also allows you to add animation to objects such as clip art images, charts and bulleted lists.

In **Slide Sorter View** you can add **Text Preset Animation** using the drop-down menu at the top of the screen.

 Click away from the slides to deselect them.

 Click Slide 2 and select, from the **Text Preset Animation** list on the Slide Sorter toolbar, **Fly From Left.** (It is currently set to **No Effect.**)

Figure 6.5: Adding text animation

 You will see the animation icon appear below that slide.

 See your changes in **Slide Show** view. You have to click the mouse or press the **Space** bar to make each line of text appear.

 Make the lines of text disappear one by one by pressing the **Backspace** key. Click the mouse to make them reappear.

Try out some of the other **Text Preset Animations.** Some of them have sounds that go with them. Try the **Camera** option as explained below.

 Select Slide 7.

 From the main menu select **Slide Show, Preset Animation.**

 Select **Camera** from the submenu.

 Try out the effect in **Slide Show View**.

Animating objects

PowerPoint will animate an object, such as a picture or chart in the same way as it will text. However, you will need to use the **Custom Animation...** dialogue box which can be complicated. The other features of Custom Animation will not be explained in this book.

 Look at Slide 5 in **Slide View**.

 From the menu, select **Slide Show, Custom Animation...**

Figure 6.6: The Custom Animation Dialogue box

On the **Effects** tab, check **Object 3**.

Click the box labelled **No Effect** and select **Fly**.

Now choose your desired **Fly** effect and sound (if any) and click **OK.**

Try it out.

Save your presentation.

The **Custom Animation** feature is more complicated than most other functions in **PowerPoint** but is fun to try out.

The best way to find out more is to try building your own presentation and experiment with different transitions, effects and animations. Give it a try!

Chapter **7**
Show Time!

In this lesson you'll be finding out how **PowerPoint** can help you during your presentation. Most of these features work best when you are giving your presentation on a big screen, and controlling it from your computer. That's when **PowerPoint** presentations are most effective.

 Open the document called **Buildings.ppt** if it is not already open.

 Select the first slide.

 Click the **Slide Show** button.

 Once in **Slide Show** mode, **right-click** the mouse and a small menu will appear.

Figure 7.1: Displaying the shortcut menu

Navigating your way around a presentation

 To find your way around a presentation you can click the **Next** and **Previous** options on the pop-up menu. This will take you to either the next or previous step in the presentation.

If you want to move to a particular slide, click **Go** on the menu. This will bring up another menu in which you select **By Title.** Go to the **Victorian** slide.

Tip:

An easier way to go to the next slide is to click the mouse button or press the **Space bar.** To go back a slide, press the **Backspace** key.

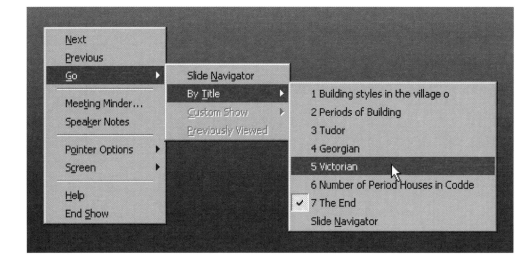

Figure 7.2: Navigation options

Using the Pen

The pen allows you to draw on the slide in freehand. This is particularly useful when explaining diagrams or graphs.

 Make sure that you are in **Slide Show** view.

 Click the right-hand mouse button and go to Slide 6, called **Number of Period Houses in Coddenham.**

Suppose you want to explain that the number of Tudor houses appears to fall at a regular rate as you move further out of the village. You can use the freehand pen to draw a trendline on the graph to help illustrate this.

 Click the right-hand mouse button again and click **Pointer Options.** Then click **Pen Color** on the pop-up menu.

 Choose **Red** or a colour that you think will show up well on the background of colours on the slide already.

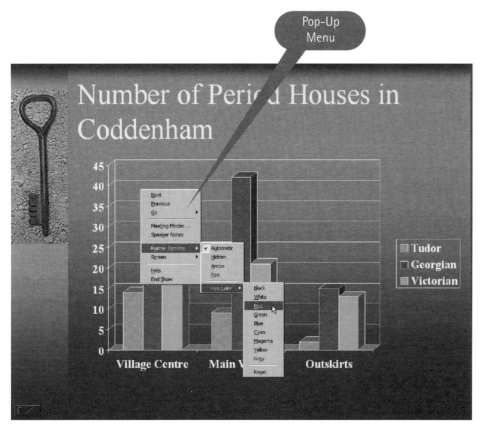

Figure 7.3: Selecting a pen colour

 Draw a trendline on your graph.

 Go to the next slide. The pen has disappeared.

 Make the pen appear again by right-clicking and selecting **Pen.**

 Experiment with different pen colours – you can draw on a single slide in many different colours!

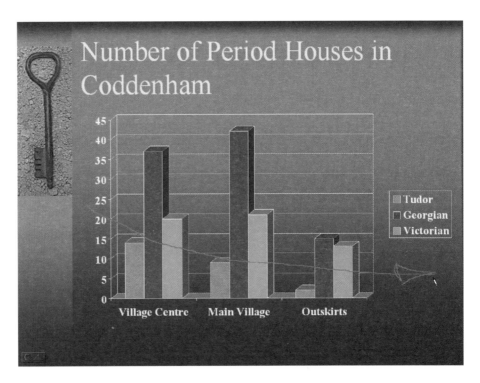

Figure 7.4: Adding freehand graphics

▶ To get rid of the pen tool, click **Pointer Options**, **Arrow** on the menu.

▶ To remove any marks you have made with the pen, right-click and select **Screen, Erase Pen** from the menu. Alternatively, press 'E'.

▶ End your slide show by clicking **End Show** on the pop-up menu, or you can press **Escape.**

▶ Clicking the **Help** option on the pop-up menu offers you a list of useful shortcuts and commands you can use in a presentation.

Figure 7.5: Useful commands

Using handouts

Handouts are often useful to help the audience run through the presentation at their own pace and for writing notes on. They can also act as reminders of the main points of your presentation.

 Make sure that you are **not** in **Slide Show** view.

 From the main menu select **File, Print.**

 From the **Print what** menu select **Handouts.**

 Select the number of slides you want to appear on each page and the order from the **Handouts** section of the Print dialogue box.

Figure 7.6: Printing handouts

 Click **OK**.

Using the Notes Pages

To assist you in your presentation you can make additional notes about each slide to prompt you. These notes are visible only by you, when you print them out or view them on screen.

 Select Slide 2, **Periods of Building**, in **Outline** view.

The pane below the slide is for adding notes. You can do this in Outline or Normal view but it is easier in Notes Page view.

 From the **View** menu select **Notes page.**

 Below the slide, type any notes that may be helpful to you when delivering your presentation.

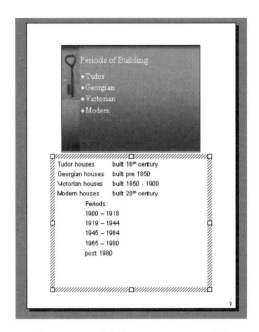

Figure 7.7: Adding notes to a slide

Viewing your notes

You can either view the notes on screen if you get stuck for words in your show or else you can print out the Notes Pages. These are similar to the Handouts pages, except that they have all your notes attached at the bottom of each page.

 Select **Slide Show View** and go to Slide **2**.

 Click the right-hand mouse button and select **Speaker Notes** to see your notes on screen.

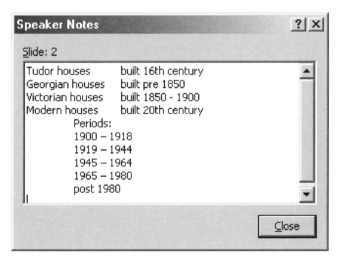

Figure 7.8: Viewing Speaker Notes during a presentation

 Press **Escape** to end your show.

Note:
In the example on the left, the text has been enlarged

Note:
You print out your Notes Pages just as for handouts! Select **Notes Pages** from the **Print What** menu.

Chapter 8
Delivery

This chapter contains tips and advice on how to deliver an effective presentation.

Presentation skills are one form of **communication skills,** and are very important all through life. They are very useful in everyday situations too, not just in front of an audience.

It is not hard to become good at presentations with a little practice and know-how.

Here are some basic tips for effective presentations to get you started.

Setting up

If you are projecting the presentation onto a wall or projector screen, you can set up the computer screen in front of you so you can see it and have the screen for the rest of the audience behind you.

Make sure the slides are readable from all seats in the room.

Rehearsals

It is a good idea to rehearse your show on your own or with your group. This will help you to time the length of the presentation and remember what you are supposed to say.

Even a quick 5-minute rehearsal can make the difference between a poor presentation and a smooth, well-timed and polished performance.

You could try rehearsing in front of a small group of friends or family to help you get used to having an audience.

Check the hardware

Arrive early to give your presentation because you need time to check the hardware. Check that you know how to operate it and that it is all working correctly.

Facing the audience

When delivering your presentation it is best not to look at the screen too often. This breaks the eye contact you will have with your audience.

 Always look at the audience and maintain **good eye contact** with them.

 Speak clearly and don't rush.

 Be **enthusiastic.** Look as though you are really enjoying giving this presentation, even if you aren't!

Audience Interaction

To keep the attention of the audience it is often a good idea to ask them simple questions about your presentation. Test their knowledge before you tell them the answer.

For example: **Can anyone tell me when Victorian times were?**

You can then reveal your answer: **Roughly 1850 to 1900.**

Another way to keep the audience involved is to provide handouts. But don't give out long handouts just before you start speaking, or people will read the handouts instead of listening to you. Plan carefully what you need to give them and when.

Appearance

Finally, look smart. A smart appearance can really make a statement. It draws people's attention towards you and helps them to take what you are saying more seriously.

This is one reason why business people wear suits to work every day. Of course, when you become as successful as Richard Branson you can wear what you like because everyone will want to hear you whatever you look like.

Kiosk presentations

You may be planning to give a live presentation using a computer or an overhead projector. Another option is to create a self-running presentation that people can view at a kiosk. These are often found at shopping malls and in entertainment complexes. You may decide to design a self-running presentation to run in the school entrance area or in a computer lab on a Parents' Day, for example.

 Make sure to have one slide selected. If no slide is selected, the following menu option will not be available.

Select **Slide Show, Slide Transition...** from the main menu. You should see the screen on the next page.

Figure 8.1: Setting up a Kiosk presentation

 From the **Advance** options click **Automatically after.** Select **5–second** intervals. Click **Apply to All**.

This will now automatically flick through the slides in your show every 5 seconds. What you now need to do is loop the presentation so that when it has finished, it starts again at the beginning.

 Click the **Slide Show** option on the main menu and select **Set Up Show...** from the submenu.

Figure 8.2: Looping your presentation

From the **Show type** category, select **Browsed at a kiosk (full screen)** from the window. Click **OK.**

This option will automatically loop the presentation until you press Escape.

 A more advanced method of setting the timings is to click the **Rehearse Timings** button in the Slide Sorter toolbar. ———————

This will record the moment you click the mouse to view the next slide or line of text.

Figure 8.3: Rehearsing the slide timings

 You can then request PowerPoint to save these timings and use them for your kiosk presentation. Give it a try.

Run your show!

Index